"Oy! Only six? Why not more?"

SIX-WORD MEMOIRS ON JEWISH LIFE

Edited by **Larry Smith**

"The brilliance is
in the brevity."

- *The New York Post*

"Six-Word
Memoirs have
been lodged in the
literary firmament."

- *Los Angeles Times*

"Will thrill
minimalists and
inspire maximalists."

- *Vanity Fair*

"You can
spend a lifetime
brainstorming."

- *The New Yorker*

"A fabulously
appealing exercise
both for writers
and for readers."

- *The Telegraph (London)*

"Larry Smith
is on a quest to
spark the creativity
of everyone."

- *Oprah Magazine*

For information on ordering books at a reduced rate for your school,
synagogue, book club, JCC or other group, contact
larry@sixwordsmith.com.

THIRD EDITION

Designer: Gail Ghezzi
Cover designed by Nicole Salzano, Jessica Busby, and Andy Mays

Library of Congress Cataloging-in-Publication Data is available upon request.

ISBN 978-0-9847350-6-8

Everyone has a story. What's yours?
www.sixwordmemoirs.com

Introduction

I f you had exactly six words to describe your life, what would they be? That's the challenge I posed on a new online platform called Twitter back in 2006. I called these short life stories "Six-Word Memoirs," a reinvention of the form that, according to literary lore, Hemingway birthed when he was challenged to write a whole novel in just six words: "For sale: baby shoes, never worn."

The Six-Word Memoir Project has since taken on a life beyond my wildest expectations. More than fifteen years and two million stories later on sixwordmemoirs.com, the six word format has become a bestselling book series and board game, a teaching tool used across the world and a powerful way to spur on self-expression for anyone and everyone. Preachers and rabbis alike have embraced six word prayers as a way to distill faith. In hospitals and veterans' groups, after-school programs and speed dating services, Six-Word Memoirs have been used to foster understanding, ease communication, and break the ice.

The six word limitation forces us to figure out the essence of who we are and what matters most. This simple form of expression can become the starting point for larger discussions. And that's exactly what we hope with this Jewish-themed chapter in the six word story, *Six-Word Memoirs on Jewish Life*. This book contains 360 Six-Word Memoirs that offer personal windows into the wild, weird, and wonderfully complex world of Judaism. We hope this book starts many conversations about the meaning of Jewish life among Jews and non-Jews alike, in synagogues and churches, among both the most Orthodox and the most secular.

"Many hands have kept me afloat," offers the writer
Nick Flynn in our first book, *Not Quite What I Was Planning:
Six-Word Memoirs by Writers Famous & Obscure*. Nick's words are
the perfect six word sentiment for a project that is the work of so
many people. First and foremost, I want to thank my partner in this
project, Reboot, a nonprofit organization whose mission is to start
discussions about Jewish identity, community, and meaning—
precisely the purpose of this book. Reboot's Roger Bennett, Tanya
Schevitz, Amelia Klein, and Dina Mann offered sage wisdom.
Reboot has brought so many wonderful people into my life,
including Amy Rothberger, who served as a valuable editor on this
book and created the glossary found in the back. If there's a word
or expression you don't know, it's most likely explained there.

Thanks also to Randy Lutterman and the JCAA, Harlene Winnick
Appelman and the Covenant Foundation, Carolyn Hessel and the
Jewish Book Council, Benjamin Maron and InterFaithFamily.com,
Morlie Levin and Birthright Israel NEXT, Jeff Newelt and *Heeb*,
Aaron Bisman, Rebecca Guber, Gary Belsky, Karen Golden,
and Melanie Abrams.

When you watch the video at **sixwordmemoirs.com/jewish**
that accompanies this book and wonder, *Where do they get that
incredible soundtrack?*, you'll know why I'm so grateful for David
Katznelson and the Idelsohn Society for Musical Preservation.
And the book's subtitle? It's the gift of prolific sixer Elisa Shevitz,
who, upon hearing of this project, exclaimed, "Oy! Only six?
Why not more?"

With each story our community becomes stronger and more
interesting. I hope you'll share your story about Jewish life or any
part of your life at **sixwordmemoirs.com**.

Larry Smith
"From this you make a living?"
Founder, Six-Word Memoirs

"My Jewish genealogy ironically reveals 'blacksmiths'."

SIX-WORD
MEMOIRS ON
JEWISH LIFE

We are not a concise people.
– Joel Stein

Newly Jewish
but an old soul.
– Erin Hoagland

Circumcision
has been least
challenging part.
– Dan Rollman

613 rules, one soul set free.
– Russ Roberts

Blonde shiksa births Jewish daughter, self.

– Amanda Keckonen Clayman

I worry if I don't worry.

– Leena Prasad

Chicken is central to the story.

– Annie Lumerman

Everything with us a question, why?

– Mark Rosenblum

In cahoots: Optometrists
and Talmud publishers.

– Rabbi Toby Manewith

Had Bar Mitzvah.
Still not man.

– Aaron Kisslinger

Everything great
came from summer camp.

– Craig Kanarick

God chose. Said no.
Now what?

– Adam Blackman

Don't count, sat in services anyway.

– Kellen Kaiser

**Jewish
star
atop our
Christmas tree.**

– A.J. Jacobs

Excessive rumination from
eating only ruminants.

– Jonathan Freund

Wait, you've got a
little schmutz.

– Michele Reznik

Half Jewish.
Half Italian.
Totally stuffed.

– Dave Cirilli

A pronounced weakness
for smoked fish.

– Adam Levy

Mourning missing out on Jewish childhood.

– Ally Reece

Wasn't expecting
to miss Hebrew school.

– Audrey Lang

Family spends meals
discussing other meals.

– Jana Loeb

**Hypocrite:
Prays to God,
uses JDate.**

– Aimee Randall

Gym teacher's son prefers
Stephen Sondheim.

– Mickey Rapkin

You're gay? L'chaim!
He's goyishe? Shonda!

– Adam Pollack

The best hair, the worst spilkes.

– Joanna Arkans

From Trochenbrod,
a renewed story unfolds.

– Esther Safran Foer

I do not stand idly by.

– Daniel Schwartz

Eight Chanukah nights.
Feels like thirty.

– *Ayelet Waldman*

Sunday night?
Yes, lobster is kosher.

– *Floyd Skloot*

"Avinu Malkeinu,"
my favorite melancholy song.

– *Angelina Love*

My grandmother's tattoo dominates my nightmares.

– *Lux Alptraum*

No sacrament. Just brisket. Take charge.

– *Rachel Gross-Prinz*

Jew in Arkansas?
Vey iz mir.

– *Amos Lassen*

From talit to tichel.
Always evolving.

– *Melissa Scholten-Gutierrez*

Prayer begins with questions
not answers.

– *Alanna Sklover*

Nazi's daughter saved
by Jewish Manhattan.

– Anna Steegmann

Rabbi's sermons are
lullabies
with meaning.

– Max Sterenson

Found my people, if not God.

– Christopher Noxon

**I kvetch.
And therefore, I am.**

– Elizabeth Kalman

Loved the food,
    hated the shiva.

– David Hirshey

The Torah's story tells me mine.

– Devorah Spilman

One Jewish book
changed the world.

– Carolyn Hessel

More Philip Roth
than David Lee.

– Charles London

Every meal is a *Seinfeld* episode.

– Karen Golden

Started off kosher. Then, discovered bacon.

– Anna Wexler

Born with big nose.
Pursued comedy.

– Andy Borowitz

Half Jewish, half Armenian: All survivor.

– Amy Keyishian

Visited Dead Sea,
returned with Life.

– John Wilder

Definitely still wandering,
    but
        not
           lost.

– Ruthie Garelik

Comedic fire:
rub two schticks together.

– Ed Small

My Judaism is somatic: blood, bone.

– Ellen Rosen

A quarter Jewish. Do I count?

– Heather Dearly

Be/t part of Judai/m: men/chy men.

– Amy Friedman

Married Christian.
Gaydar works, Jewdar broken.

– Michael Forster Rothbart

The Manischewitz made me do it.

– Maya Stein

I'm the Messiah...

so are You.

– Amichai Lau-Lavie

My grandparents got out.
I'm here.

– Erika Dreifus

Chopping liver, telling jokes.
Too schmaltzy?

– Dan Fost

Suspended disbelief for the Bar Mitzvah.

– Neil Fine

Mom: "Jewish boys don't play football."

– Michael Areinoff

**Sick of sharing
birthday with Jesus.**

– Cathy Alter

Big Jewish fish.
Small gentile pond.

– David Baum

Live,
lose,
learn,
love,
laugh: L'chaim!

– Susan Barnes

Family tree:
lots of zaftig women.

– Vicki Botnick

Children breathing in my Jewish heart.

– Mark Horowitz

Goy says "Oy!"
after meeting family.

– Drew Brockington

Gay Jew puts
Judy in Judaism.

– *Michael Getty*

"Finish eating...people starving in Europe."

– *Stephanie Andelman*

Tikkun Olam.
Gemilut Chasadim.
Mel Brooks.

– *Ian Zaback*

Prostate hurts from all the grief.

– *Gary Shteyngart*

Ate too much,
prayed too little.

– Jennifer Small

Traditions to transmit:
God, not guilt.

– Matthue Roth

Impressive Hasidic lineage. Dating a Catholic.

– Aliza Bartfield

**Overstuffing is part
of my aesthetic.**

– Bill Bragin

Jew by choice
findſ her voice.

– Gwen Wexler

I like Palestinians. Get over it.

– Sara Gunning

The Torah's God:
a bipolar adolescent.

– Michael Castleman

Paying retail is against
my religion.

– Jennifer Baron

No way to escape the mishegas.

– Jackie Leventhal

Oh, right.
This too shall pass.

– Adene Sacks

Jesus may save, but Moses invests.

– Mel Alper

Sorry, I can't stop feeding you.

– Naomi Adiv

Taught children;
  now they teach me.

– Ron Burton

**Mani. Schvitz. Manischewitz.
Rinse, lather, repeat.**

– Emily Hirshey

Tunisian Sephardi rejected for NAACP scholarships.

– *Erik Levis*

Living Torah means always
    having gratitude.

– *Jeremy Rovinsky*

Vermont Jew:
sukkah in a parka.

– *Renee Woliver*

From this you make a living?

– *Sophie Rosenblum*

I should have
had the chicken.

– Larry David

"Putz! Schmuck! Noodnik! Nebbish!"
"Sheket, Dad!"

– Jim Gladstone

Have faith in asking many questions.

– Rachel Kramer Bussel

Former monochromatic wardrobe
now seeking color.

– Yaakov Hellinger

Smash that glass,
tap that ass.

– Sheri Knauth

Adam Sandler, update your Chanukah list.

– Laura Horwitz

"Your voice sounds thinner **today, darling."**

– Abby Ellin

Preserve the past.
Be the future.

– Shauna Waltman

Yid dish is a kosher meal.

– Al Jaffee

When life meets Torah,
blessings emerge.

– Jen Gubitz

Constantly balancing
between
visits, guilt trips.

– Meredith Sires

Shiksa wife more Jewish than me.

– Andy Goodman

Covenant: blessing and burden. My choice.

– Natalie Pullen

It's different. And I like that.

– Nicole Goldstein

To Florida! Annual migration with birds.

– Jim Berman

Lapsed, cultural, and now professional Jew.

– Michael Kaminer

Leviticus: Love your neighbor as yourself.

– Rabbi Seth Adelson

Be a mensch; pass it on.

– Marsha Stein

I can't;
I have a blister.

– Daniel Okrent

Shabbat:
Eight Jews,
twelve dietary restrictions.

– Jamie Levine Daniel

Learned my Judaism
at pro-choice rally.

– Rabbi Sari Laufer

Free will:
God plans, man laughs.

– Yael Roberts

Plowing our texts for pertinent meaning.

– Christopher Orev Reiger

**Latkethon at my mother's
gynecologist's home.**

– Erica Fishbein

**Jews in
groups make
me nervous.**

– Gary Belsky

Protocols, shmotocols. Just gimme the Zion.

– Gideon Lichfield

One RV mezuzah.
Two wandering Jews.

– Amy Beth Oppenheimer

Bat Mitzvah. Menstruation.
Same day?
Womanhood!

– Amanda Chudnow

Thought Yiddish.
Married British.
Oy! Oi!

– Rachel Pine

Baruch Ata Adonai Elohainu… um… uh….

– Mary McConnell

Like Zusya,
trying to be me.

– Rabbi Steven Rubenstein

At 55, considering a Bat Mitzvah.

– Cheryl Corson

Is he Jewish?
Is he Jewish?

– *Shoshana Berger*

What's most Jewish is my atheism.

– *Molly Crabapple*

Lubavitch Chabadnik asks: "Jewish?"
Me: "No."

– *Douglas Rushkoff*

God, are you with me now?

– *Nicola Behrman*

My identity but not my politics.

– Naomi Levy

**Born Orthodox Jew.
Now Orthodox cynic.**

– Molly Bee

Never fulfilled Bat Mitzvah
speech expectations.

– Robin Beth Schaer

Trans, Jewish. Don't need a mohel.

– Mel King

**One subject,
endless opinions,
all talk.**

– *Lesley Stein*

Jewish vegetarian:
Only miss gefilte fish.

– *Hilary Bothma*

**Thought God punished.
I was wrong.**

– *Josh Radnor*

Repairing world:
until Messiah, our job.

– *Elaine Lavine*

Why worry?
History suggests it's advisable.

– Dinah Finkelstein

God giveth.
God taketh away.
Goddamnit.

– Jacob Berkman

Davening. An introduction to early sciatica.

– Rich Shadrin

**Hid comics
inside Hebrew school
textbooks.**

– Jeff Newelt

I wonder about God.
Truth? Fiction?

– Ben Greenman

**Webcast Yom Kippur services.
Strangely satisfying.**

– Amy Ramos

Guilty overachiever
seeking spirituality
and
patience.

– Judith Rose

Torah wellsprings
   water my parched soul.

– Blumi Mishulovin

Living the truth that all's *echad*.

– Marni Rothman

Woody Allen is my personal lullaby.

– Jeni Janson

Used up my six words
complaining.

— *Michelle Wolfson*

**Endless vista,
always present,
usually hidden.**

— *David Glickman*

Choice through knowledge —
your steps alone.

— *Aimee Weiss*

World
is
narrow
bridge,
be
brave!

— *Marci Bellows*

No, not related.
Horowitz: Judaism's "Smith."

– *Adam Horowitz*

"House of bondage" jokes, funny annually.

– *Rachel Sklar*

**I'll bet Jesus
found the afikomen.**

– *Steven Wolfe*

Mom and God had boundary issues.

– *Marty Kaplan*

You never write,

you never call.

– Susan Silver

Tikkun Olam
is my raison d'être.

– Melissa Reitkopp

**Build a better world.
No excuses.**

– Matt Fieldman

Six years old; puked on Masada.

– Rachel Shukert

Breast milk is pareve.
Weird kashrut.

– Abigail Greenbaum

This is a Roman nose, OK?

– Jason Biggs

Eat, Love, Pray;
Eat, Love;
Eat.

– Fred Scherlinder Dobb

**See, Mom,
I'm a doctor. (Ph.D.)**

– Jerry Heyman

At least you know he's circumcised.

– Amy Schumer

I'm a Jew. Joke, I do.

– Abby Kuhns

Crosses don't work
on Jewish vampires.

– Satya Tretiak

Our inheritance:
Gratitude.
Unrest.
Humility.
Audacity.

– Rabbi Sharon Brous

Judaism: Tradition, innovation messily rolled together.

– *Sara Steinman*

God is in
the
small details.

– *Shanni Profesorsky*

Less oy. More joy. Learn. Celebrate.

– *Deborah Lipstadt*

I use chutzpah
as an aphrodisiac.

– *Amy Rothberger*

Deli food always
beats
fine dining.

– *Rozzie Heeger*

Chicken soup!
With or without kreplach?

– *Dr. Alan M. Reznik*

Pastrami is the spice of life.

– *Avi Flamholz*

**Love the food,
hate the sanctimony.**

– *Norman Wilner*

Putting *some* pep in my *s*chlep.

– *Ashley Allen*

Rogachev, Harbin, Havana,
Sydney, Philadelphia,
Next?

– *Amelia Klein*

I was in need.
Heard: Hineini.

– *Elissa Froman*

Traditional sederists.
Culinary matzachists. Passover *chazers.*

– *Samuel Basch*

Chicken fat
makes life worth living.

– *Jane and Michael Stern*

Wait, is your kippah actually edible?

– *Aaron Laurito*

An intense love affair with God!

– JoAnne Shapiro

They got paté. We got ptcha.

– Mark Lamster

Presbyterian school rebel, Hollywood shabbos-keeper.

– Rob Kutner

Saying Kaddish. Missing you. Remembering. Remembering.

– Debra Darvick

I discovered myself
through being Jewish.

– Sarah Ducker

Youth group, camp, Israel,
rabbinate, family.

– Greg Kanter

Nobody told my hormones
I'm Orthodox.

– Eliana Block

Mother, our lady of perpetual dissatisfaction.

– Jennifer Glick

– *Liana Finck*

We're not arguing.
We're aggressively agreeing.

– Josh Gondelman

Shakespeare Shmakespeare;
we've got Philip Roth!

— *Raymond Simonson*

**Threat of extinction breeds
Jewish excellence.**

— *Tovah Feldshuh*

My grandma
would be so proud.

— *Greg Clayman*

Judaism accesses
fuller humanity positive,
negative.

— *Beth Kissileff*

**Million,
million,
million,
million,
million,
million?**

– Hadassah Gross

Judaism:
5,000 years of terrible candy.

– *Gail Lerner*

You were right Mom, it matters.

– *Mitzi Druss*

Strong opinion, biting humor,
warm heart.

– *Lori Warren*

Christmas:
Thank God for Chinese restaurants.

– *Tamara Straus*

Only keep kosher in the diaspora.
– *Mara Berman*

I need more
Bar Mitzvah money.
– *Jack Grubman*

Hindu Jew seeks light
in everything.
– *Marc Mannheimer*

Real bagels don't
have jalapeño peppers.
– *Paul Beckman*

Jewish summer camp, my *etz chayim*.

– Ari J. Shapiro

**Texas Bar Mitzvah.
Bacon-wrapped shrimp.**

– Jeremy Goldberg

Neurotic Jew
neurotic about her neuroses.

– Danielle Sherman

Half Jewish.
Sadly, not Lenny Kravitz.

– Max Bachhuber

Gedolei Yisrael: Fonzie, Hyman, Kaminsky, Konigsberg.

– *Tony Michels*

German-Jews. Dyslexia. Acting. Family. Writing. Complete.

– *Henry Winkler*

**Raised Arkansas Baptist.
Now Detroit Jew.**

– Gayla Bassham

Thought "klutz" was term
of endearment.

– Jacqueline Rice

**Family disappointment?
My hatred of lox.**

– Robin Gelfenbien

Six words,
six hundred thirteen opinions.

– Bryan Kort

Neurotic hypochondriac
seeks medical attention,
please.

– Jessica Lester

Not exactly Chosen. More like inducted.

– Coleen Goodson

Genesis, Exodus, Leviticus,
Numbers, ummmm, Duderroneous.

– Rabbi Stephen Landau

Hair: liability turned asset; still thick.

– Ben Falik

Gluten-free life is Passover year round.

– *Naomi Jill Wolf*

Old parchment scrolls
soothe weary souls.

– *Michael J. Sullivan*

**Apocalypse is when
pickles run out.**

– *Paul Ratner*

Question everything.
Eat everything. Feel bad.

– *Jenji Kohan*

I thought I caught a gefilte!

– *Ryan Eastman*

I've learned I'm really more Jew-*ish*.

– *Dana Kader Robb*

Others have history; we have memory.

– *Alexandra Benjamin*

Did you call your mother today?

– *Lisa Soble Siegmann*

We bonded over our deviated septums.

– Alessandra Rizzotti

Black gay ex-Christian woman
now Jewish.

– Erika Davis

Dim sum is our Sunday school.

– Liza Wyles

Shoah shadows.
Vibrant life.
Hopeful future.

– Rachel Dubelu

Favorite Jewish ballplayers:
Greenberg, Koufax and...

– *Louis Smith*

Wondering: Madonna helping or hurting us?

– *The Sklar Brothers*

**Carbohydrates
call my name every day.**

– *Mary Petersdorf*

Love people always.
Rest is commentary.

– *Joelle Novey*

613 rules, who has the koach?

– Hadass Segal

Do good.
Be kind.
Thank God.

– Anita Diamant

**Lightbulb needs changing.
Call a handyman.**

– Amy Feldman

**Uncle Saul's commandment:
"Meals need seltzer!"**

– Gail Ghezzi

Sh'ma Yisrael Adonai
Eloheinu Adonai Echad.

– Deuteronomy

The Sh'ma,
my favorite six words.

– Xander Karsten

Bar Mitzvah video

used as blackmail.

– *Jon Papernick*

Chosen for something.
Not sure what...
– *Adam Clyne*

Yes,
I'm wearing a sweater,
Mom.
– *Mikey Franklin*

**Romantic Jewess wishes
Chanukah featured mistletoe.**
– *Elisa Shevitz*

"But you just don't look Jewish."
– *Elizabeth Wurtzel*

Not shomer Shabbat.
Too much homework.

– Sarah Rubock

Israel means "to wrestle."
Explains everything.

– Tiffany Shlain

I am always filled with angst.

– Juliet Simmons

The hora is the best part.

– Gillian Zoe Segal

Coolest kid at Yeshiva. Still nerdy.

– Jason Klein

We embrace tradition
but reject convention.

– Edward Harwitz

**My Tikkun Olam
includes your enemies.**

– Sharon McKellar

Bring a date to my shiva.

– Steven Liss

Thanks for the blue eyes, Cossacks.

– Lisa Brown

Read right
to left
for him.

– Lindsey Digangi

Secret law:
Maine Jews allowed lobster.

– Joel Rubin

Obligation and responsibility:
ennobling Jewish concepts.

– Ruth Messinger

Haggled.
Mistaken for Jewish.
Tremendously flattered.

– Laureatte Loy

Cooking chicken soup stirs
mother memories.

– Carol Smith

School bully throwing Bac-Os at Jews.

– Leonard White

Black Jew,
both outsiders
even here.

– Walter Mosley

Read Marx, Freud,
Talmud; still reading.
– Anne Schiff

Haggadah:
most radical book there is.
– Jonathan Safran Foer

I fantasize about
Avigdor from Yentl.
– Jessica Berlin

Enough tsuris to fill six books.
– Rose Waldman

Kissed a lady. Said shehecheyanu later.

– Elissa Vinnik

Choosing to be chosen, best choice.

– Sarah Belknap

I'd prefer more gelt than guilt.

– Patricia Carragon

Got my nose done. (Still circumcised.)

– Michael Malice

Rabbi accidentally spoke of
"Shitting siva."

– Jo-Ellen Balogh

Post-denominational Jews eat Thai for Christmas.

– Shari Salzhauer Berkowitz

Skiing?
A person could get hurt.

– Arnold Simon

Film professor quandary:
screen Woody Allen?

– Jonathan Sherman

Zayde refuses to die
without great-grandchildren.

— *Leslie Stonebraker*

**Lost Judaism; found again.
I'm home.**

— *Deborah Adler*

Will eat bacon but refuses ham.

— *Max Baumgarten*

A life uncriticized is not Jewish.

— *Lisa Wurtele*

What page are we on again?

– Matthew Sheren

Got allowance.
Saved, spent,
gave tzedakah.

– Lisa Exler

Tattooed Jew seeks
entrance to Heaven.

– Elijah Aroha

Didn't know, started learning, still questioning.

– Debra Nussbaum Cohen

Remember where you're from.
And going.

– Artie Gold

Reason Jews joke:
life not funny.

– Howard Jacobson

**Thought Easter
was a zombie story.**

– Daniel Handler

Oh no, Oh no, Oh no.

– Maira Kalman

Wanna be righteous,
instead just anxious.

– Jill Soloway

Read, struggle,
discuss, resolve,
rinse, repeat.

– Jason Menayan

Converted to Judaism for the jokes.

– Lorenzo Mattozzi

Walter: "I don't roll on Shabbos!"

– The Big Lebowski

**Yiddish makes even
pleasantries sound filthy.**

– *Karen Sulkis*

For sale. Pair tefillin. Never worn.

– *Roger Bennett*

Never accept gift horses.
Not kosher.

– *Paul Harrington*

I glory in my Jewish traditions.

– *Mayor Ed Koch*

Secret latke ingredient is knuckle blood.

– Rachel Fershleiser

**Shehecheyanu over garden tomato.
I'm Jewish.**

– Lisa Colton

Jewish model,
not a model Jew.

– Joshua Feldman

Oy.
So much room
for interpretation.

– Betsy Polk Joseph

Legacy of strong women in family.

– *Joanne Brockington*

Seeing God's face in your face.

– *Rabbi Laura Geller*

Don't know which Self to synopsize.

– *Art Spiegelman*

**My son: half-Christian,
half-Jewish, mostly Jewish.**

– *Rachel Axler*

I have a fetish for altakockers.

– *Amy Sohn*

**Half-Jewish: circumcised,
but circumspect about it.**

– *George Held*

Today's puny teens,
tomorrow's **Jewish leaders**.

– *Karen Katzoff*

The guilt threats
mobilize family gatherings.

– *Rebecca Guber*

Observant means paying
very careful attention.

– Sharon Price

**I wrestle with God.
Every day.**

– Cori Mancuso

Perpetually longing for place in community.

– Dara Wilensky

Can't talk;
my hand is broken.

– Ellen Ullman

Displaced dad makes
smoked meat sandwich.

– Hal Niedzviecki

**Guilty admission:
didn't hate Hebrew school.**

– Jackie Miller

Books change lives.
They've changed mine.

– Joseph Telushkin

Who couldn't use a little Shabbat?

– Terri Ginsberg Bernsohn

Grew up in Texas.
Shalom y'all.

– Dayna Shaw

The Mamaloshen is in my heart.

– Dina Mann

Reason not dogma,
joy not fear.

– Amy Cohen

"Dad, six Jewish words?"
"Enough, Sandi!"

– Sandi DuBowski & Elliot DuBowski

Om Shalom:
Best of both worlds.

– Jeff Greenwald

Funky brown chick
throws Chanukah party.

– Twanna Hines

Faith is fine,
service fills souls.

– JJ Slatkin

Bacon brings me closer to God.

– Ray Richmond

Catching and releasing "nice Jewish boys."

– Lisa Bottone

Prefer mechitza minyan for the eye-candy.

– Ira Stup

Comic with guarenteed work on Christmas.

– Ophira Eisenberg

Baruch atah Adonai, viva Puerto-Rico ha'olam.

– Venessa Hidary

Born Mayflower descendent.
Avraham new ancestor.

– Marty Johnston

The comfort of so many questions.

– Linda Bernstein

Shalom.
That's such a great word.

– Josephine Collett

Proud Diasporans write
new history chapter.

– Jordana Horn

**They didn't kill us.
Let's eat!**

– Eileen Cukier

Ohio Orthodox equals
New York reform.

– Stan Friedman

Divine memoir:
Let there be light.

– Natalie Wood

Everybody knows one of your relatives.

– Joyce Gordon

Comedy, brains,
and belly to spare.

– *Laurel Felt*

G-d listens to a sound argument.

– *Sandra Little*

Nondairy creamer?
Effing kosher industrial complex.

– *Dory Kornfeld*

There's NO hole in the sheet!

– *Jillian Scheer*

I know, I know. The Holocaust.

– Judah Ariel

Table of ten,
          one bottle:
                    dayenu.

– Robin Epstein

**A smorgasbord of genetic diseases.
Hooray!**

– David Wolkin

Treif dishes are for pepperoni
pizza.

– Lynn Goldberg

Not cool to scapegoat a Jew.

– Terri Kay Emanuel

Beautiful traditions I wish were mine.

– Kimberly Shepherd

**My first hangover:
post Bar Mitzvah.**

– Mark Dommu

Covenant matters.
Set example.
Judaism endures.

– Monnie Newman

Perpetually joining JDate.
Perpetually canceling JDate.

– Adri Cowan

I hope he finds neurotic erotic.

– Liz Nord

I guess I'd always been
rabbi-curious.

– Lynn Harris

Not all Jewish boys are nice.

– *Michael Lucas*

Life is to dance Hava Nagila.

– *David Katznelson*

Connection with my people, not shul.

– *Deborah Sweet Kucinski*

Belong to something
bigger than me.

– *Amy Amiel*

Found Jewish princess.
Goodbye, succulent pork.

– Leah Damski

We read backward but think forward.

– Deborah Copaken Kogan

God said, "Do this."
Now what?

– Michael Kates

I was Jewish in another life.

– Don Letta

**No hell, really?
What a rip-off!**

– *Sascha Rothchild*

I'm going to worry about it.

– *Buck Henry*

Yalla, choose what
works for you.

– *Oren Goldenberg*

No, Bubbe,
    I'm not married yet.

– Gary Rozman

Looking for my b'shert.
You him?

– Robyn Faintich

Read *Portnoy's Complaint*, swore off liver.

– Lynn LeBlanc

In Hebrew, six words are ten.

– Janice Silverman Rebibo

Sixteen Rachels
in my address book.

– Larry Smith

"You don't wear a little hat?"

– Jaron Berliner

My people celebrate life every day.

– Elena Levitt

My number ends in 613.
Coincidence?

– Jeremy Tofler

I'm sick of talking about Jews.

– *Shalom Auslander*

Only writing this out of guilt.

– *David Sax*

Funny hats,
funny curls,
funny jokes.

– *Dick Pasky*

Still no clue. But tryin'.
L'chaim.

– *Margie Howe*

Anxiety, trauma:
but make it cute.

– Jessie Kahnweiler

Jewish romance full of Easter Eggs.

– Melanie Abrams

birth
bris
bed
bath
and
beyond

Zeks verter iz badir a mayse?
(By you six words is a story?)

– Eddy Portnoy

**Unsure of God?
You're cool here.**

– Emilia Diamant

Life finally converging
with absolute glee.

– Ali Adler

**Kugel. Comedy. Kvetching.
Questioning. Welcome home.**

– Alysia Reiner

A wandering Jew
never says
goodbye.

– *Richard Davis*

A Glossary of Terms & Phrases

613 The number of mitzvot, or commandments, written in the Torah.

Afikomen The piece of matza hidden during the Passover seder. Usually children will search for it, and a prize is awarded to the child who finds it first.

Altakockers Yiddish term for old folks.

Avinu Malkeinu Literally: "Our Father, Our King." Refers to a well-known prayer of supplication said on and between Rosh Hashanah and Yom Kippur.

Baruch Ata Adonai Eloheinu The opening words of a Hebrew blessing. Translated as: "Blessed art thou, oh Lord our God."

B'shert One's destined mate or spouse; meant to be.

Bubbe Grandmother.

Chazers Literally: pigs. Idiomatically, people who are sloppy or greedy.

Davening Praying, often in a swaying or back-and-forth rocking motion.

Dayenu Refrain from a song in the Passover seder meaning "enough!"

Echad Hebrew word meaning "one."

Etz Chayim A Hebrew phrase that literally translates to "tree of life."

Gedolei Yisrael A Hebrew phrase meaning "the greats of Israel," used to describe the most revered thinkers or leaders of a generation, generally referring to rabbis.

Gefilte [Fish] Ashkenazi delicacy made of various kinds of ground fish. "Delicacy" tends to be a subjective term depending on one's palate.

Gemilut Chasadim Acts of righteousness. It is said that a good life is one of Torah, Mitzvot (commandments) and acts of righteousness.

Goy Yiddish word meaning "non-Jewish person," sometimes derogatory. Plural: goyim, adjective: goyish/goyishe.

Hineini Word meaning, "Here I am." It is said by Adam, Abraham and Moses in conversation with God to declare their presence, and is often used in modern-day Yom Kippur services and sermons.

Kaddish A prayer recited as part of the Jewish mourning rituals, following the passing of a loved one.

Kashrut/Kosher Jewish dietary laws. Often referred to as "keeping kosher."

Kippah Skull cap/head covering traditionally worn by men. Also called "yarmulke."

Koach Strength.

Kreplach Meat-filled dumpling often eaten in chicken soup.

Kvetch Yiddish word meaning to gripe or complain.

L'chaim Hebrew meaning "To life!" Used as exclamation in lieu of "cheers!"

Mamaloshen Yiddish term meaning "mother tongue" that refers to the Yiddish language.

Mechitza Partition in traditional synagogues used to separate the men's and women's sections.

Mensch Yiddish word for a good, upstanding person, usually a man.

Mezuzah Scroll hung on the doorposts of Jewish homes, containing the words of the *Sh'ma* (see below).

Minyan The ten-person minimum required to pray in a group service. Idiomatically refers to the service itself.

Mishegas Yiddish term meaning craziness. Idiomatically, also means business or fussiness.

Mohel Person who performs ritual circumcisions.

Pareve Term which implies a food has neither meat nor dairy designation.

Plotz Yiddish term meaning to collapse, faint or keel over in response to strong emotion (excitement, disappointment, surprise, exhaustion, etc.).

Ptcha Savory gelled dish made from bones (often calves feet), flavored with garlic and other spices.

Schmutz Yiddish word for filth or dirt.

Schvitz Literally: to sweat. A schvitz can also be a steam room or bath house.

Shabbat/Shabbos Sabbath day of rest.

Shehecheyanu Blessing said the first time one performs a given act.

Shiksa Yiddish term for non-Jewish woman, sometimes derogatory in its connotation.

Shiva The ritual seven-day mourning period where the bereaved are visited by friends, family and community members.

Schlep Yiddish word for to carry, haul, or trek in an inconvenient fashion.

Sh'ma Prayer translated as "Hear O Israel, the Lord our God, the Lord is One."

Schmaltzy Sentimental or sappy; overly kitschy. Derived from *schmaltz*, which literally translates to "rendered chicken fat."

Shoah Hebrew term for the Holocaust.

Shomer Shabbat The practice of keeping and observing the laws of the Sabbath.

Shonda An outrage, a shame, or a pity; a scandal.

Shul Yiddish term for synagogue.

Spilkes/Shpilkes Yiddish equivalent of "ants in your pants" — anxiety, jumpiness. Can stem from excitement or apprehension.

Sukkah An outdoor hut constructed to re-enact the temporary dwellings the Israelites lived in while wandering in the desert.

Talit A prayer shawl traditionally worn by men during morning services. In progressive streams of Judaism, sometimes also worn by women.

Tefillin Black leather box and straps worn (generally by men) during morning weekday prayers that contain scrolls with the text of the *Sh'ma*.

Tichel Head covering worn by religious women once they are married.

Tikkun Olam Concept of repairing the world through acts of community service, social justice, environmental action and other imperatives.

Treif Yiddish word for non-kosher.

Tsuris Yiddish word for problems or issues of worry/concern.

Tzedakah Literal meaning: righteousness or justice. Refers to charity.

Vey iz mir Yiddish term meaning "woe is me." Often follows "Oy" and is a term of exasperation.

Yarmulke Head covering traditionally worn by men. Also called "kippah."

Zaftig Having a full or shapely figure.

Zayde Grandfather.

Zusya Refers to Rabbi Zusya of Hanipol, the protagonist of a famous story which culminates in him saying, "When I die and go to the world to come, they will not ask me, 'Zusya, why were you not Moses?' They will ask me, 'Zusya, why were you not Zusya?'"

Say it in Six!

Since the Six-Word Memoir® made its debut in 2006, more than two million short life stories have been shared on the world's largest short-form personal storytelling platform, sixwordmemoirs.com. In classrooms and boardrooms, churches and synagogues, veterans' groups and across the dinner table, Six-Word Memoirs have become a powerful tool to catalyze conversation, spark imagination, or simply break the ice.

Share your Six-Word Memoir at **www.sixwordmemoirs.com.**

   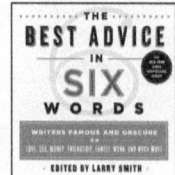 

Want This Book?

This book is published with the support of the nonprofit, Reboot (rebooting.com) and available in select bookstores and online at sixwordmemoirs.com/six-store.

Interested in a discounted large order? Contact **larry@sixwordmemoirs.com** and let's talk!

About **Six -Word Memoirs**

Founded in 2007 by Larry Smith, The Six-Word Memoir Project is a bestselling series of ten books, calendar, board game, live event series, and global phenomenon. For more information, visit **www.sixwordmemoirs.com.**

Six-Word Memoir founder Larry Smith has spoken on the power of storytelling, self-expression, and community engagement at TEDx, PopTech, SXSW Interactive, Summit Series, AARP'S 50+ convention, and elsewhere. He has led team-building sessions at companies including Netflix, Dell, Levi's, OhioHealth, Nationwide, JPMorgan Chase, Yelp, Google, and Shutterfly, as well as at foundations, nonprofits, synagogues, JCCs, and schools across the world.

About Reboot

Reboot is an arts and culture nonprofit that reimagines and reinforces Jewish thought and traditions. As a premier research and development platform for the Jewish world, Reboot catalyzes its network of preeminent creators, artists, entrepreneurs, and activists to produce experiences and products that evolve the Jewish conversation and transform society. All Reboot projects imagine Jewish ritual and tradition afresh, offering an inviting mix of discovery, experience, and reflection through events, exhibitions, recordings, books, films, DIY activity toolkits, and apps. These projects have engaged more than 5.5 million participants in the past five years and continue to inspire Jewish connections and meaning by encouraging participants to become creators in their Jewish experience.
Find out more at **Rebooting.com.**